Great Works | Instructional Guides for Literature

LORD of the FLIES

A guide for the novel by William Golding
Great Works Author: Jennifer Kroll

SHELL EDUCATION

Publishing Credits

Corinne Burton, M.A.Ed., *Publisher*; Emily R. Smith, M.A.Ed., *Content Director*; Lee Aucoin, *Senior Graphic Designer*; Dana Strong, *Editor*; Stephanie Bernard, *Associate Editor*; Courtney Roberson, *Senior Graphic Designer*

Image Credits

All images Shutterstock.

Standards

© 2007 Teachers of English to Speakers of Other Languages, Inc. (TESOL)
© 2014 Board of Regents of the University of Wisconsin System, on behalf of WIDA—www.wida.us
© Copyright 2010. National Governors Association Center for Best Practices and Council of Chief State School Officers. All rights reserved.
ISTE Standards for Students, ©2016, ISTE® (International Society for Technology in Education), iste.org. All rights reserved.
© Copyright 2007–2017 Texas Education Association (TEA). All rights reserved.
Shell Education

Shell Education

A division of Teacher Created Materials
5301 Oceanus Drive
Huntington Beach, CA 92649-1030
http://www.tcmpub.com/shell-education
ISBN 978-1-4807-8516-8
© 2018 Shell Educational Publishing, Inc.
Printed in USA. WOR004

Table of Contents

How to Use This Literature Guide

Today's standards demand rigor and relevance in the reading of complex texts. The units in this series guide teachers in a rich and deep exploration of worthwhile works of literature for classroom study. The most rigorous instruction can also be interesting and engaging!

Many current strategies for effective literacy instruction have been incorporated into these instructional guides for literature. Throughout the units, text-dependent questions are used to determine comprehension of the book as well as student interpretation of the vocabulary words. The books chosen for the series are complex exemplars of carefully crafted works of literature. Close reading is used throughout the units to guide students toward revisiting the text and using textual evidence to respond to prompts orally and in writing. Students must analyze the story elements in multiple assignments for each section of the book. All these strategies work together to rigorously guide students through their study of literature.

The next few pages will make clear how to use this guide for a purposeful and meaningful literature study. Each section of this guide is set up in the same way to make it easier for you to implement the instruction in your classroom.

Theme Thoughts

The great works of literature used throughout this series have important themes that have been relevant to people for many years. Many of the themes will be discussed during the various sections of this instructional guide. However, it would also benefit students to have independent time to think about the key themes of the novel.

Before students begin reading, have them complete *Pre-Reading Theme Thoughts* (page 13). This graphic organizer will allow students to think about the themes outside the context of the story. They'll have the opportunity to evaluate statements based on important themes and defend their opinions. Be sure to have students keep their papers for comparison to the *Post-Reading Theme Thoughts* (page 64). This graphic organizer is similar to the pre-reading activity. However, this time, students will be answering the questions from the point of view of one of the characters in the novel. They have to think about how the character would feel about each statement and defend their thoughts. To conclude the activity, have students compare what they thought about the themes before they read the novel to what the characters discovered during the story.

How to Use This Literature Guide (cont.)

Vocabulary

Each teacher overview page has definitions and sentences about how key vocabulary words are used in the section. These words should be introduced and discussed with students. There are two student vocabulary activity pages in each section. On the first page, students are asked to define the ten words chosen by the author of this unit. On the second page in most sections, each student will select at least eight words that he or she finds interesting or difficult. For each section, choose one of these pages for your students to complete. With either assignment, you may want to have students get into pairs to discuss the meanings of the words. Allow students to use reference guides to define the words. Monitor students to make sure the definitions they have found are accurate and relate to how the words are used in the text.

On some of the vocabulary student pages, students are asked to answer text-related questions about the vocabulary words. The following question stems will help you create your own vocabulary questions if you'd like to extend the discussion.

- How does this word describe _____'s character?
- In what ways does this word relate to the problem in this story?
- How does this word help you understand the setting?
- In what ways is this word related to the story's solution?
- Describe how this word supports the novel's theme of . . . .
- What visual images does this word bring to your mind?
- For what reasons might the author have chosen to use this particular word?

At times, more work with the words will help students understand their meanings. The following quick vocabulary activities are a good way to further study the words.

- Have students practice their vocabulary and writing skills by creating sentences and/or paragraphs in which multiple vocabulary words are used correctly and with evidence of understanding.
- Students can play vocabulary concentration. Students make a set of cards with the words and a separate set of cards with the definitions. Then, students lay the cards out on the table and play concentration. The goal of the game is to match vocabulary words with their definitions.
- Students can create word journal entries about the words. Students choose words they think are important and then describe why they think each word is important within the novel.

How to Use This Literature Guide *(cont.)*

Analyzing the Literature

After students have read each section, hold small-group or whole-class discussions. Questions are written at two levels of complexity to allow you to decide which questions best meet the needs of your students. The Level 1 questions are typically less abstract than the Level 2 questions. Level 1 is indicated by a square, while Level 2 is indicated by a triangle. These questions focus on the various story elements, such as character, setting, and plot. Student pages are provided if you want to assign these questions for individual student work before your group discussion. Be sure to add further questions as your students discuss what they've read. For each question, a few key points are provided for your reference as you discuss the novel with students.

Reader Response

In today's classrooms, there are often great readers who are below-average writers. So much time and energy is spent in classrooms getting students to read on grade level that little time is left to focus on writing skills. To help teachers include more writing in their daily literacy instruction, each section of this guide has a literature-based reader response prompt. Each of the three genres of writing is used in the reader responses within this guide: narrative, informative/explanatory, and argument. Students have a choice between two prompts for each reader response. One response requires students to make connections between the reading and their own lives. The other prompt requires students to determine text-to-text connections or connections within the text.

Close Reading the Literature

Within each section, students are asked to closely reread a short section of text. Since some versions of the novels have different page numbers, the selections are described by chapter and location, along with quotations to guide the readers. After each close reading, there are text-dependent questions to be answered by students.

Encourage students to read each question one at a time and then go back to the text and discover the answer. Work with students to ensure that they use the text to determine their answers rather than making unsupported inferences. Once students have answered the questions, discuss what they discovered. Suggested answers are provided in the answer key.

How to Use This Literature Guide (cont.)

Close Reading the Literature (cont.)

The generic, open-ended stems below can be used to write your own text-dependent questions if you would like to give students more practice.

- Give evidence from the text to support . . . .

- Justify your thinking using textual evidence about . . . .

- Find evidence to support your conclusions about . . . .

- What textual evidence helps the reader understand . . . ?

- Use the book to tell why _____ happens.

- Based on events in the story, ...

- Use textual evidence to describe why . . . .

Making Connections

The activities in this section help students make cross-curricular connections to writing, mathematics, science, social studies, or the fine arts. Each of these types of activities requires higher-order thinking skills from students.

Creating with the Story Elements

It is important to spend time discussing the common story elements in literature. Understanding the characters, setting, and plot can increase students' comprehension and appreciation of the story. If teachers discuss these elements daily, students will more likely internalize the concepts and look for the elements in their independent reading. Another important reason for focusing on the story elements is that students will be better writers if they think about how the stories they read are constructed.

Students are given three options for working with the story elements. They are asked to create something related to the characters, setting, or plot of the novel. Students are given a choice in this activity so that they can decide to complete the activity that most appeals to them. Different multiple intelligences are used so that the activities are diverse and interesting to all students.

How to Use This Literature Guide *(cont.)*

Culminating Activity

This open-ended, cross-curricular activity requires higher-order thinking and allows for a creative product. Students will enjoy getting the chance to share what they have discovered through reading the novel. Be sure to allow them enough time to complete the activity at school or home.

Comprehension Assessment

The questions in this section are modeled after current standardized tests to help students analyze what they've read and prepare for tests they may see in their classrooms. The questions are dependent on the text and require critical-thinking skills to answer.

Response to Literature

The final post-reading activity is an essay based on the text that also requires further research by students. This is a great way to extend this book into other curricular areas. A suggested rubric is provided for teacher reference.

Correlation to the Standards

Shell Education is committed to producing educational materials that are research and standards based. As part of this effort, we have correlated all of our products to the academic standards of all 50 states, the District of Columbia, the Department of Defense Dependents Schools, and all Canadian provinces.

Purpose and Intent of Standards

The Every Student Succeeds Act (ESSA) mandates that all states adopt challenging academic standards that help students meet the goal of college and career readiness. While many states already adopted academic standards prior to ESSA, the act continues to hold states accountable for detailed and comprehensive standards. Standards are statements that describe the criteria necessary for students to meet specific academic goals. They define the knowledge, skills, and content students should acquire at each level. State standards are used in the development of our products, so educators can be assured they meet state academic requirements.

How to Find Standards Correlations

To print a customized correlation report of this product for your state, visit our website at **www.teachercreatedmaterials.com/administrators/correlations/** and follow the online directions. If you require assistance in printing correlation reports, please contact our Customer Service Department at 1-877-777-3450.

Correlation to the Standards (cont.)

Standards Correlation Chart

The lessons in this guide were written to support today's college and career readiness standards. This chart indicates which sections of this guide address which standards.

College and Career Readiness Standard	Section
Read closely to determine what the text says explicitly and to make logical inferences from it; cite specific textual evidence when writing or speaking to support conclusions drawn from the text.	Analyzing the Literature Sections 1–5; Reader Response Sections 1–5; Close Reading the Literature Sections 1–5
Determine central ideas or themes of a text and analyze their development; summarize the key supporting details and ideas.	Analyzing the Literature Sections 1–5
Analyze how and why individuals, events, or ideas develop and interact over the course of a text.	Analyzing the Literature Sections 1–5; Reader Response Sections 1–5
Interpret words and phrases as they are used in a text, including determining technical, connotative, and figurative meanings, and analyze how specific word choices shape meaning or tone.	Vocabulary Sections 1–5
Analyze the structure of texts, including how specific sentences, paragraphs, and larger portions of the text (e.g., a section, chapter, scene, or stanza) relate to each other and the whole.	Analyzing the Literature Sections 1–5; Creating with the Story Elements Sections 1–5; Post-Reading Response to Literature
Assess how point of view or purpose shapes the content and style of a text.	Analyzing the Literature Sections 1–5; Reader Response Sections 1–5; Post-Reading Response to Literature
Write arguments to support claims in an analysis of substantive topics or texts using valid reasoning and relevant and sufficient evidence.	Reader Response Sections 1–5; Close Reading the Literature Sections 1–5; Post-Reading Response to Literature
Write informative/explanatory texts to examine and convey complex ideas and information clearly and accurately through the effective selection, organization, and analysis of content.	Reader Response Sections 1–5; Post-Reading Response to Literature
Write narratives to develop real or imagined experiences or events using effective technique, well-chosen details and well-structured event sequences.	Reader Response Sections 1, 3–4; Culminating Activity 1
Produce clear and coherent writing in which the development, organization, and style are appropriate to task, purpose, and audience.	Reader Response Sections 1–5; Creating with the Story Elements Sections 1–5; Culminating Activity 1–2
Draw evidence from literary or informational texts to support analysis, reflection, and research.	Analyzing the Literature Sections 1–5; Reader Response Sections 1–5; Close Reading the Literature Sections 1–5
Write routinely over extended time frames (time for research, reflection, and revision) and shorter time frames (a single sitting or a day or two) for a range of tasks, purposes, and audiences.	Reader Response Sections 1–5; Creating with the Story Elements Sections 1–5; Culminating Activity 1–2; Post-Reading Response to Literature

Correlation to the Standards (cont.)

Standards Correlation Chart (cont.)

College and Career Readiness Standard	Section
Evaluate a speaker's point of view, reasoning, and use of evidence and rhetoric.	Making Connections Section 2; Post-Reading Response to Literature
Make strategic use of digital media and visual displays of data to express information and enhance understanding of presentations.	Creating with the Story Elements Sections 1–5; Culminating Activity 2
Adapt speech to a variety of contexts and communicative tasks, demonstrating command of formal English when indicated or appropriate.	Reader Response Sections 1–5; Creating with the Story Elements Sections 1–5
Demonstrate command of the conventions of standard English grammar and usage when writing or speaking.	Analyzing the Literature Sections 1–5; Reader Response Sections 1–5; Close Reading the Literature Sections 1–5; Culminating Activity 1; Post-Reading Response to Literature
Demonstrate command of the conventions of standard English capitalization, punctuation, and spelling when writing.	Analyzing the Literature Sections 1–5; Reader Response Sections 1–5; Close Reading the Literature Sections 1–5; Culminating Activity 1; Post-Reading Response to Literature
Determine or clarify the meaning of unknown and multiple-meaning words and phrases by using context clues, analyzing meaningful word parts, and consulting general and specialized reference materials, as appropriate.	Vocabulary Sections 1–5

TESOL and WIDA Standards

The lessons in this book promote English language development for English language learners. The following TESOL and WIDA English Language Development Standards are addressed through the activities in this book:

- **Standard 1:** English language learners communicate for social and instructional purposes within the school setting.

- **Standard 2:** English language learners communicate information, ideas and concepts necessary for academic success in the content area of language arts.

About the Author—William Golding

William Gerald Golding was born in 1911 in Cornwall, England. As a boy, he attended the school where his father taught. Golding then attended Oxford University where he initially studied science at his father's urging. After two years, however, he began to study literature instead, his true area of interest. Golding graduated from Oxford in 1935 and worked for four years as a writer, actor, and producer with a small theater. In 1939, he married Ann Brookfield. The couple had two children together. In 1939, Golding also began teaching English and philosophy at Bishop Wordsworth's School in Salisbury, England. However, he took a leave from his teaching position in 1940 to join the Royal Navy during World War II. Golding spent five years in the navy and was deeply affected by this experience. He was involved in active combat and was present off the French coast during the D-Day invasion. After the war, Golding returned to his teaching post at Bishop Wordsworth's School. He wrote *Lord of the Flies* while teaching there. He continued teaching until 1961 when he left to pursue a full-time writing career.

Lord of the Flies, Golding's first novel, was published in 1954 after having been initially rejected by over twenty publishers. The novel was not an immediate success, selling only about 3,000 copies in the United States before going out of print in 1955. Shortly thereafter, however, interest in the book began to surge, and by the early 1960s, *Lord of the Flies* had become required reading in many high schools and colleges. Golding followed up *Lord of the Flies* with more than a dozen other published works, including the novels *The Inheritors* (1955), *Pincher Martin* (1956), *The Spire* (1964), *The Pyramid* (1967), and *Darkness Visible* (1979), which won the James Tait Black Memorial Prize. Golding's most ambitious work, a trilogy of novels collectively called *The Sea Trilogy*, details the emotional and moral growth of a young man undertaking an 1812 sea voyage to Australia. The first book of the trilogy, *Rites of Passage* (1980), won the Booker-McConnell Prize. William Golding went on to be awarded the Nobel Prize for Literature in 1983. He was knighted in 1988. Golding died in Cornwall in 1993.

Possible Texts for Text Comparisons

Some of William Golding's other novels include *The Inheritors*, *Pincher Martin*, *Free Fall*, and *The Spire*. In addition to his novels, Golding also wrote a play, *The Brass Butterfly*, and two collections of essays titled *The Gates* and *A Moving Target*.

Book Summary of *Lord of the Flies*

During wartime, a group of boys find themselves on an uninhabited island after a plane crash. With no adults present, the boys explore the island, which is filled with fruit trees and wild pigs. They elect a boy named Ralph as chief. The boys use a conch shell to call assemblies and pass it to take turns speaking. Piggy, an overweight, asthmatic boy with glasses, is abused verbally, but becomes a sort of advisor to Ralph. The boys use Piggy's glasses to light a signal fire, which they hope will facilitate rescue. They build shelters, though Ralph, accompanied by Simon, a "batty" boy prone to fainting, does most of the work. Later, a ship passing near the island fails to stop because the boys on fire duty have let the fire die. Ralph chastises the others for ignoring rules set up for the good of the group. The younger boys express fear that a Beast may live on the island. The older boys try to reassure the younger ones. However, when a parachuted corpse lands on the mountain peak, it is mistaken for the Beast. Fear and tension grows.

Jack attempts to overthrow Ralph. When the others refuse to vote Ralph out, Jack creates a rival camp. He and his followers kill a pig and put its head on a stick. Jack offers a feast to all who join his "tribe." Meanwhile, Simon hallucinates that the staked pig's head is speaking to him. Following his seizure, he discovers the paratrooper corpse and recognizes it for what it is. He heads to Jack's feast to tell the others, but when he crawls out of the jungle, they mistake him for the Beast and kill him. Not long after, Jack raids Ralph's camp to steal Piggy's glasses. Ralph, Piggy, and the twins, Samneric, head to Jack's fort to demand the return of the glasses. There, the boys have a spat and begin to chase after Ralph. Luckily, Ralph runs into a naval officer who will take the boys back to civilization, but not without the realization of their loss of innocence.

Cross-Curricular Connection

Although not overtly a war novel, *Lord of the Flies* seems to have been inspired, at least in part, by events of World War II. The novel can be taught to students who have recently studied or are currently studying this war. It can also be taught to students studying psychology, and can be used to illustrate or spark discussion about issues of group and evolutionary psychology.

Possible Texts for Text Sets

- Ballantyne, R. M. 2017. *The Coral Island*. CreateSpace Independent Publishing Platform.
- Dashner, James. 2010. *The Maze Runner*. Delacorte Press. New York.
- Pratchett, Terry. 2009. *Nation*. HarperCollins. New York.
- Ransome, Arthur. 2010. *Swallows and Amazons*. David R. Godine Publisher. Boston.
- Stevenson, Robert Louis. 2017. *Treasure Island*. Millennium Publications. South Kingstown.
- Wyss, Johann D. 2009. *The Swiss Family Robinson*. Puffin Books. New York.

Name _____

Date _____

Pre-Reading Theme Thoughts

Directions: Read each of the statements in the first column. Decide if you agree or disagree with the statements. Record your opinion by marking an *X* in Agree or Disagree for each statement. Explain your choices in the fourth column. There are no right or wrong answers.

Statement	Agree	Disagree	Explain Your Answer
Those perceived as different are more likely to be picked on and become scapegoats.			
Children by nature are not moral. They need adults to teach and reinforce moral behavior.			
In the absence of laws and social structures, human beings will slip into a state of cruel savagery.			
Honesty is the best policy.			

Teacher Plans

Vocabulary Overview

Ten key words from this section are provided below with definitions and sentences about how the words are used in the book. Choose one of the vocabulary activity sheets (pages 15 or 16) for students to complete as they read this section. Monitor students as they work to ensure the definitions they have found are accurate and relate to the text. Finally, discuss these important vocabulary words with students. If you think these words or other words in the section warrant more time devoted to them, there are suggestions in the introduction for other vocabulary activities (page 5).

Word	Definition	Sentence about Text
scar (ch. 1)	a rocky outcrop	The boys climb up over the **scar** as they explore the island.
motif (ch. 1)	a dominant feature or idea	The beach where the boys land is interrupted by a square **motif** of granite.
specious (ch. 1)	something that seems possible but is not the case; misleading	The tide pool has the **specious** appearance of being deep when it actually is not.
effulgence (ch. 1)	radiance or brightness	The hot sun reflecting on the lagoon has blinding **effulgence**.
decorous (ch. 1)	polite and restrained; in good taste	Even when he's excited, Piggy behaves in a **decorous** manner.
mortification (ch. 1)	humiliation or shame	Jack blushes with **mortification** when Ralph is elected leader of the group.
immured (ch. 1)	enclosed or confined against one's will	While climbing the hill, the boys become **immured** in a tangle of vines.
ebullience (ch. 2)	cheerfulness and energy	Piggy is more serious and less full of **ebullience** than most of the other boys.
officious (ch. 2)	filled with authority, but in an annoying or domineering way	While trying to light the fire, the boys shout instructions at one another in **officious** voices.
recrimination (ch. 2)	accusation in response to accusation from someone else	Piggy has a tone of **recrimination** in his voice when he picks up the conch and speaks.

Name _____

Date _____

Understanding Vocabulary Words

Directions: The following words appear in this section of the book. Use context clues and reference materials to determine an accurate definition for each word.

Word	Definition
scar (ch. 1)	
motif (ch. 1)	
specious (ch. 1)	
effulgence (ch. 1)	
decorous (ch. 1)	
mortification (ch. 1)	
immured (ch. 1)	
ebullience (ch. 2)	
officious (ch. 2)	
recrimination (ch. 2)	

Name _____

Date _____

During-Reading Vocabulary Activity

Directions: As you read these chapters, record at least eight important words on the lines. Try to find interesting, difficult, intriguing, special, or funny words. Your words can be long or short. They can be hard or easy to spell. After each word, use context clues in the text and reference materials to define the word.

- _____
- _____
- _____
- _____
- _____
- _____
- _____
- _____
- _____
- _____

Directions: Respond to these questions about the words in this section.

1. What does the word **scar** mean as it is used in these chapters?

   _____
   _____
   _____

2. Which of the boys is described as behaving in a **decorous** manner, and what does that mean?

   _____
   _____
   _____
   _____

Analyzing the Literature

Provided below are discussion questions you can use in small groups, with the whole class, or for written assignments. Each question is given at two levels so you can choose the right question for each group of students. Activity sheets with these questions are provided (pages 18–19) if you want students to write their responses. For each question, a few key discussion points are provided for your reference.

Story Element	■ Level 1	▲ Level 2	Key Discussion Points
Setting	How do the boys come to be on the island? Based on what you've read so far, will it be easy or hard to survive and why?	Why do you think the author had the boys' plane land on an island? What challenges do the boys face in a world without adults?	The boys' plane is shot down. It isn't hard to survive on an island because food, fresh water, and shelter are usually plentiful. People can usually put aside their differences to survive, but without that to unite them, cracks will form. Isolation and leadership struggles are some of the challenges the boys face.
Characters	How does Piggy differ from the other boys, either physically or in his opinions and views?	Discuss the qualities in Piggy that set him apart from the other boys. How is he more like a grownup or more connected to civilization than the others?	Piggy is overweight, wears glasses, and has asthma. He seems the least comfortable in the natural setting, the most conscious of its dangers, and most focused on returning to civilization. He wants to organize the group with the conch and by collecting a roster of names.
Plot	How do the boys use the conch shell? How does Ralph's possession of the conch affect his position in the group?	Explain the role of the conch shell, what it represents, and why it is important to the group of boys.	The conch shell is viewed by Piggy as a valuable object. Later, it becomes a symbol of democratic social order. The boys call meetings by blowing on the conch. They pass it to take turns talking. Ralph's ownership of the conch secures his position as elected group leader.
Characters	Does Ralph seem like a good or bad person? How do you feel about his treatment of Piggy?	List Ralph's character strengths and weaknesses. How do you feel about his treatment of Piggy?	Ralph's repeated "sucks to your auntie/ass-mar" comments to Piggy are unkind, and he betrays Piggy by divulging his detested nickname. However, he shows leadership potential as he reassures and organizes the group.

Name _____

Date _____

■ Analyzing the Literature

Directions: Think about the section you just read. Read each question, and state your response with textual evidence.

1. How do the boys come to be on the island? Based on what you've read so far, will it be easy or hard to survive and why?

_____

_____

_____

_____

2. How does Piggy differ from the other boys, either physically or in his opinions and views?

_____

_____

_____

_____

_____

3. How do the boys use the conch shell? How does Ralph's possession of the conch affect his position in the group?

_____

_____

_____

_____

_____

4. Does Ralph seem like a good or bad person? How do you feel about his treatment of Piggy?

_____

_____

_____

_____

_____

_____

Name _____

Date _____

▲ Analyzing the Literature

Directions: Think about the section you just read. Read each question, and state your response with textual evidence.

1. Why do you think the author had the boys' plane land on an island? What challenges do the boys face in a world without adults?

    _____

    _____

    _____

    _____

2. Discuss the qualities in Piggy that set him apart from the other boys. How is he more like a grownup or more connected to civilization than the others?

    _____

    _____

    _____

    _____

    _____

3. Explain the role of the conch shell, what it represents, and why it is important to the group of boys.

    _____

    _____

    _____

    _____

    _____

4. List Ralph's character strengths and weaknesses. How do you feel about his treatment of Piggy?

    _____

    _____

    _____

    _____

    _____

    _____

Name _____

Date _____

Reader Response

Directions: Choose one of the following prompts about this section to answer. Be sure you include a topic sentence in your response, use textual evidence to support your opinion, and provide a strong conclusion that summarizes your opinion.

Writing Prompts

- **Narrative Piece**—Describe a time when you were without adult supervision for an extended period of time. How did you feel about being on your own? What happened? Compare and contrast your experience and feelings with that of the boys in the first two chapters of *Lord of the Flies*.
- **Argument Piece**—Who would make the best leader: Ralph, Jack Merridew, or Piggy? Why?

_____

_____

_____

_____

_____

_____

_____

_____

_____

_____

_____

_____

_____

_____

_____

_____

_____

Name _____

Date _____

Close Reading the Literature

Directions: Closely reread the section in chapter 1 where Jack Merridew is introduced. Start with the sentence, "Within the diamond haze of the beach something dark was fumbling along." Continue until you read, "Jack stood up." Read each question, and then revisit the text to find evidence that supports your answer.

1. Select a sentence from the text that tells you something about the relationship between Jack and the other choir members. What inferences can you make from it?

   _____

   _____

   _____

2. What words and phrases are used to describe Jack's physical appearance? What can you infer about his personality based on the description of his appearance?

   _____

   _____

   _____

3. Why doesn't Piggy try to ask the names of the choir members and remember them? How does he feel about Jack? Explain how the text helped you draw these conclusions.

   _____

   _____

   _____

4. Do you think Piggy and Jack are more likely to become friends or enemies? What about Ralph and Jack? Include textual evidence from this passage to support your answers.

   _____

   _____

   _____

   _____

Name _____

Date _____

Making Connections–Foreshadowing and Predictions

Author William Golding uses foreshadowing in the first two chapters of *Lord of the Flies*. Foreshadowing is a literary device in which the author hints at events that are to come later in the narrative.

Directions: Answer the questions below on another sheet of paper to make predictions about events that you think may occur later in the novel.

The Boulder

1. In chapter 1, the boys push a large rock down from the top of the mountain. Why do they do this?

2. What role, if any, might falling boulders play later in the novel?

The Piglet

3. At the end of chapter 1, Ralph and Jack encounter a trapped piglet. Based on what happens in this passage, what role do you think pigs might play later in the novel?

Piggy's Glasses

4. How do the boys use Piggy's glasses?

5. What role do you think the glasses will play later in the novel?

6. What might happen to the glasses, and what makes you think so?

The Fire

7. Why do the boys light a fire, and what happens when they do?

8. What role do you think fire may play later in the novel?

Name _____

Date _____

Creating with the Story Elements

Directions: Thinking about the story elements of character, setting, and plot in a novel is very important to understanding what is happening and why. Complete **one** of the following activities based on what you've read so far. Be creative and have fun!

Characters

Create a set of five illustrated character profile cards, one for each of the following characters Ralph, Piggy, Jack Merridew, Sam and Eric (can have one card for both twins), and Simon. Include the following headings on each of the cards: *Physical Appearance, Approximate Age, Character's Strengths, Character's Weaknesses, Character Least Likely To…,* and *Character Most Likely To…* Use the text of *Lord of the Flies* and your imagination to fill in the profile information on each card. Include an illustration of each character on the reverse side of the card.

Setting

Draw a map of the island. Base your illustration on the descriptive details provided in the first two chapters of *Lord of the Flies*. Label the various parts of the island. Use color coding to represent different surfaces (sand, water, rock, vegetation).

Plot

Using the hints offered in the text and your imagination, create a newspaper front page that includes stories about the events that have resulted in the boys becoming stranded on the island.

Teacher Plans

Vocabulary Overview

Ten key words from this section are provided below with definitions and sentences about how the words are used in the book. Choose one of the vocabulary activity sheets (pages 25 or 26) for students to complete as they read this section. Monitor students as they work to ensure the definitions they have found are accurate and relate to the text. Finally, discuss these important vocabulary words with students. If you think these words or other words in the section warrant more time devoted to them, there are suggestions in the introduction for other vocabulary activities (page 5).

Word	Definition	Sentence about Text
festooned (ch. 3)	adorned, as with ribbons or other decorations	The trees, beneath which Jack lurks, are described as **festooned** with creepers.
furtive (ch. 3)	attempting to avoid notice, often in order to stay out of danger or trouble	Startled by a bird's cry, Jack reacts more like a **furtive** creature than an aggressive hunter.
inscrutable (ch. 3)	something that cannot be seen through and is confusing	Jack cannot see through the **inscrutable** mass of creepers covering the trail.
vicissitudes (ch. 3)	sudden changes of luck or circumstance, generally negative	Jack is frustrated by the **vicissitudes** of his day of hunting and his inability to catch a pig.
contrite (ch. 3)	feeling remorse or guilt	Simon seems **contrite** when he makes a mistake and the shelter he is building with Ralph collapses.
detritus (ch. 4)	waste or debris	Tiny creatures scavenge for food in the **detritus** of the island's tide pools.
footling (ch. 4)	trivial and irritating	Ralph is annoyed by Piggy's **footling** comments about the possibility of rescue.
effigy (ch. 5)	a sculpture or model of a person	The littlun named Percival is silent at first and stands looking like an **effigy** of a miserable person.
decorum (ch. 5)	correct or proper behavior	Piggy is shocked out of his usual **decorum** when he hears the odd thing Simon is saying.
discursive (ch. 5)	passing aimlessly from one subject to another; digressive; rambling	The organized assembly breaks up, and the boys begin their own **discursive** conversations.

Name _____

Date _____

Understanding Vocabulary Words

Directions: The following words appear in this section of the book. Use context clues and reference materials to determine an accurate definition for each word.

Word	Definition
festooned (ch. 3)	
furtive (ch. 3)	
inscrutable (ch. 3)	
vicissitudes (ch. 3)	
contrite (ch. 3)	
detritus (ch. 4)	
footling (ch. 4)	
effigy (ch. 5)	
decorum (ch. 5)	
discursive (ch. 5)	

Name _____

Date _____

During-Reading Vocabulary Activity

Directions: As you read these chapters, record at least eight important words on the lines. Try to find interesting, difficult, intriguing, special, or funny words. Your words can be long or short. They can be hard or easy to spell. After each word, use context clues in the text and reference materials to define the word.

- _____
- _____
- _____
- _____
- _____
- _____
- _____
- _____
- _____

Directions: Respond to these questions about the words in this section.

1. Which characters are described as **furtive**, and what are they doing when described that way?

   _____
   _____
   _____
   _____

2. How does Ralph feel when Piggy makes **footling** comments about building sundials and being rescued?

   _____
   _____
   _____
   _____

Analyzing the Literature

Provided below are discussion questions you can use in small groups, with the whole class, or for written assignments. Each question is given at two levels so you can choose the right question for each group of students. Activity sheets with these questions are provided (pages 28–29) if you want students to write their responses. For each question, a few key discussion points are provided for your reference.

Story Element	■ Level 1	▲ Level 2	Key Discussion Points
Plot	How and why do the boys fail to follow the rules that have been set? What are the consequences?	What signs are there that the social structure of the group is breaking down? How and why are the boys becoming more "primitive"?	The boys have not been filling the coconut shells with water or helping build the shelters. The hunters abandon fire duty to hunt. The fire represents hope of rescue and a return to civilization. Jack has to "think for a moment" before he can even remember what "rescue" is.
Character	How can wearing a mask change a person's behavior or personality? Who paints on a mask in this section and why?	Why does Jack paint on the mask? What signs are there that this change of external appearance might affect him internally?	Students can be prompted to discuss times when they may have changed their behavior while wearing a costume or mask. In the novel, Jack paints his face in the hope that this camouflage will help him succeed at the hunt. His behavior shifts when he dons the mask. He begins to dance crazily and snarl, "appalling" the others.
Setting	Do you think there is really a beast living on the island? If not, what is causing the boys to imagine a beast?	Ralph tries to reassure the boys that there is no beast living on the island. How and why does Jack undermine Ralph's message?	The idea of a "beastie" seems to stem from the nightmares of "littluns" and has to do with a feeling of unsafety in the absence of adults. Ralph tries to squelch "beastie" fears. Instead of stating definitively that there is no beast, Jack offers to protect the boys by killing it.
Characters	How do the boys feel about the fact that they've killed a pig? Do you think you would feel the same way?	What emotions do the boys feel as they reenact the pig's death? How does their reenactment make you feel? Why?	The boys are proud of themselves. They delight in reenacting the kill. No sympathy for the animal is expressed. Students may say that the reenactment with its "kill the pig" chant is shocking. They may say that the boys' behavior makes them feel uneasy.

Name _____

Date _____

Analyzing the Literature

Directions: Think about the section you just read. Read each question, and state your response with textual evidence.

1. How and why do the boys fail to follow the rules that have been set? What are the consequences?

   _____

   _____

   _____

   _____

   _____

2. How can wearing a mask change a person's behavior or personality? Who paints on a mask in this section and why?

   _____

   _____

   _____

   _____

   _____

3. Do you think there is really a beast living on the island? If not, what is causing the boys to imagine a beast?

   _____

   _____

   _____

   _____

   _____

4. How do the boys feel about the fact that they've killed a pig? Do you think you would feel the same way?

   _____

   _____

   _____

   _____

   _____

Name _____

Date _____

▲ Analyzing the Literature

Directions: Think about the section you just read. Read each question, and state your response with textual evidence.

1. What signs are there that the social structure of the group is breaking down? How and why are the boys becoming more "primitive"?

_____

_____

_____

_____

_____

2. Why does Jack paint on the mask? What signs are there that this change of external appearance might affect him internally?

_____

_____

_____

_____

_____

3. Ralph tries to reassure the boys that there is no beast living on the island. How and why does Jack undermine Ralph's message?

_____

_____

_____

_____

_____

4. What emotions do the boys feel as they reenact the pig's death? How does their reenactment make you feel? Why?

_____

_____

_____

_____

_____

Name _____

Date _____

Reader Response

Directions: Choose one of the following prompts about this section to answer. Be sure you include a topic sentence in your response, use textual evidence to support your opinion, and provide a strong conclusion that summarizes your opinion.

Writing Prompts

- **Argument Piece**—If you were stranded on the island with the boys, which character would you most likely choose to befriend? Why? Which would you least likely choose to befriend? Why?
- **Informative/Explanatory Piece**—Compare and contrast Ralph and Jack. How have their differences of focus driven a wedge between them in these chapters?

_____

_____

_____

_____

_____

_____

_____

_____

_____

_____

_____

_____

_____

_____

_____

_____

_____

_____

Name _____

Date _____

Close Reading the Literature

Directions: Closely reread the section in chapter 4 describing the interactions of the boys on the beach. Start with the sentence, "Roger and Maurice came out of the forest." Continue until you read, "Then Henry lost interest in stones and wandered off." Read each question, and then revisit the text to find evidence that supports your answer.

1. Why does Maurice run away after getting sand in Percival's eye? What can you infer about him based on his actions here?

   _____
   _____
   _____
   _____

2. Find the description of Roger's physical appearance. What can you tell about his personality based on this description? Point to specific words and phrases from the description that seem most significant.

   _____
   _____
   _____
   _____

3. Why does Roger throw stones at Henry, and why does he miss? Cite the text to support your answer.

   _____
   _____
   _____

4. Would you predict the boys' treatment of one another is likely to improve, worsen, or remain the same as weeks go by? Cite events from the passage that helped you draw this conclusion.

   _____
   _____
   _____

Name _____

Date _____

Making Connections–Quotable Characters

Directions: Find a quotation from each character below that you feel best sums up his personality, interests, and focus. Write the quotation, and explain why you selected it.

Piggy

_____

_____

_____

I chose this quotation because…

_____

_____

_____

Ralph

_____

_____

_____

_____

I chose this quotation because…

_____

_____

_____

Jack

_____

_____

_____

I chose this quotation because…

_____

_____

_____

Name _____

Date _____

Creating with the Story Elements

Directions: Thinking about the story elements of character, setting, and plot in a novel is very important to understanding what is happening and why. Complete **one** of the following activities based on what you've read so far. Be creative and have fun!

Characters

Make an organizational chart representing the group of boys stranded on the island. The chart should show visually how the characters relate to each other. You may choose to use varied shapes or color coding to represent alliances and/or the different types of characters, such as "littluns," older boys, leaders, and followers.

Setting

Create a travel brochure for the island. Include photographs or drawings, as well as brief descriptions of sites to see and things to do.

Plot

Rewrite the assembly scene from chapter 5 as either a dramatic play or reader's theater play. Bonus: Act out your play with classmates, or read it aloud with friends and record your reading.

Vocabulary Overview

Ten key words from this section are provided below with definitions and sentences about how the words are used in the book. Choose one of the vocabulary activity sheets (pages 35 or 36) for students to complete as they read this section. Monitor students as they work to ensure the definitions they have found are accurate and relate to the text. Finally, discuss these important vocabulary words with students. If you think these words or other words in the section warrant more time devoted to them, there are suggestions in the introduction for other vocabulary activities (page 5).

Word	Definition	Sentence about Text
interminable (ch. 6)	unending; annoyingly long	The dawn seems **interminable** to the boys as they wait for the light of day.
tremulously (ch. 6)	shaking or trembling from fear or nervousness	The twins cling to each other **tremulously** after mistaking the dead paratrooper for a beast.
embroiled (ch. 6)	involved in a conflict	Piggy feels uncomfortable about becoming **embroiled** in the conflict between Ralph and Jack.
constrainedly (ch. 6)	stiffly or uneasily	Lost in his own anguished thoughts, Ralph can only smile **constrainedly** at Simon.
leviathan (ch. 6)	a sea monster or any huge marine animal	Ralph imagines that a **leviathan** is under the water breathing in and out.
coverts (ch. 7)	thickets giving shelter to wild animals or game	Ralph tries not to think that the beast might be hiding in the ferny **coverts**.
scurfy (ch. 7)	covered with scaly matter	The skin of the boys has become **scurfy** with salt from bathing in the sea.
traverses (ch. 7)	places where someone can travel or cross over	The boys climb across rocky **traverses** where they have to use both their hands and feet.
impervious (ch. 7)	impossible to penetrate or affect	Roger, who communicates poorly and shows little emotion, seems **impervious** to Ralph.
bravado (ch. 7)	a swaggering display of courage; reckless or pretended bravery	Ralph shows **bravado** when he declares that he will go up the mountain to look for the beast.

Name _____

Date _____

Understanding Vocabulary Words

Directions: The following words appear in this section of the book. Use context clues and reference materials to determine an accurate definition for each word.

Word	Definition
interminable (ch. 6)	
tremulously (ch. 6)	
embroiled (ch. 6)	
constrainedly (ch. 6)	
leviathan (ch. 6)	
coverts (ch. 7)	
scurfy (ch. 7)	
traverses (ch. 7)	
impervious (ch. 7)	
bravado (ch. 7)	

Name _____

Date _____

During-Reading Vocabulary Activity

Directions: As you read these chapters, record at least eight important words on the lines. Try to find interesting, difficult, intriguing, special, or funny words. Your words can be long or short. They can be hard or easy to spell. After each word, use context clues in the text and reference materials to define the word.

- _____
- _____
- _____
- _____
- _____
- _____
- _____
- _____
- _____
- _____

Directions: Now, organize your words. Rewrite each of the words on a sticky note. Work with a group to create a bar graph of your words. Stack any words that are the same on top of one another. Different words should appear in different columns. Finally, discuss with the group why certain words were chosen more often than other words.

Analyzing the Literature

Provided below are discussion questions you can use in small groups, with the whole class, or for written assignments. Each question is given at two levels so you can choose the right question for each group of students. Activity sheets with these questions are provided (pages 38–39) if you want students to write their responses. For each question, a few key discussion points are provided for your reference.

Story Element	■ Level 1	▲ Level 2	Key Discussion Points
Plot	What arrives from the "world of grownups" at the beginning of chapter 6? What does this arrival tell us about that world?	Why is the dead paratrooper significant to the boys and in a larger context? What human tendencies does he represent?	The boys receive a disturbing sign that the grownup world is in violent turmoil. The paratrooper might be said to represent the human tendency to separate into enemy "tribes" and go to war.
Character	Describe Simon. How is he different from the other boys?	What sets Simon apart from other boys in the group? Point to any unusual things that he does or says.	The other children see Simon as crazy or "batty." Simon predicts Ralph's survival. He seems to enjoy being alone in nature and is unafraid to head off through the forest alone. He does not believe in the beast. Students may recall his suggestion that the "beast" is "maybe only us."
Setting	What and where is "the castle"? Does it seem to be more of a frightening or an exciting place? Why?	Compare and contrast Ralph's and Jack's feelings about "the castle." What can we tell about them from their responses to the setting?	"The castle" is a "narrow ledge of rock, a few yards wide and perhaps fifteen long," jutting out into the sea. The height, rockiness, and idea that it might be a beast's lair make it frightening. Ralph, who is interested in safety and survival, calls it a "rotten place." Jack sees it as a good place to have a fort.
Plot	Does fear usually make human beings behave better or worse? How might fear affect the behavior of the boys in the future?	Describe how fear can have a positive or negative impact on human behavior. Predict what might happen as the characters become more fearful.	Students may argue that fear can cause people to behave selfishly, engage in scapegoating and violence, and fail to stand up for what is right, while those who overcome fear may act in heroic ways for the greater good. Students may predict that the boys' fear will lead to tragedy.

Name _____

Date _____

Analyzing the Literature

Directions: Think about the section you just read. Read each question, and state your response with textual evidence.

1. What arrives from the "world of grownups" at the beginning of chapter 6? What does this arrival tell us about that world?

   _____

   _____

   _____

   _____

2. Describe Simon. How is he different from the other boys?

   _____

   _____

   _____

   _____

   _____

3. What and where is "the castle"? Does it seem to be more of a frightening or an exciting place? Why?

   _____

   _____

   _____

   _____

   _____

4. Does fear usually make human beings behave better or worse? How might fear affect the behavior of the boys in the future?

   _____

   _____

   _____

   _____

   _____

   _____

Name _____

Date _____

▲ Analyzing the Literature

Directions: Think about the section you just read. Read each question, and state your response with textual evidence.

1. Why is the dead paratrooper significant to the boys and in a larger context? What human tendencies does he represent?

   _____

   _____

   _____

   _____

2. What sets Simon apart from other boys in the group? Point to any unusual things that he does or says.

   _____

   _____

   _____

   _____

   _____

3. Compare and contrast Ralph's and Jack's feelings about "the castle." What can we tell about them from their responses to the setting?

   _____

   _____

   _____

   _____

4. Describe how fear can have a positive or negative impact on human behavior. Predict what might happen as the characters become more fearful.

   _____

   _____

   _____

   _____

   _____

   _____

Name _____

Date _____

Reader Response

Directions: Choose one of the following prompts about this section to answer. Be sure you include a topic sentence in your response, use textual evidence to support your opinion, and provide a strong conclusion that summarizes your opinion.

Writing Prompts

- **Narrative Piece**—Describe a time when you felt truly afraid. Compare and contrast your experience with that of the boys as described in chapters 6 and 7 of *Lord of the Flies*.
- **Argument Piece**—Argue that the boys are safer or less safe on the island than they would be in the "world of grownups." In your response, make sure you mention the "sign…from the world of grownups" that the boys receive at the beginning of chapter 6.

_____

_____

_____

_____

_____

_____

_____

_____

_____

_____

_____

_____

_____

_____

_____

_____

_____

Name _____

Date _____

Close Reading the Literature

Directions: Closely reread the section of the boar encounter and its reenactment in chapter 7. Start with the sentence, "The bushes crashed ahead of them." Continue until you read, "Ralph sat up." Read each question, and then revisit the text to find evidence that supports your answer.

1. How does his attempt to spear a boar affect Ralph? Does it change how he feels about himself or about hunting? Explain how the text helped you draw these conclusions.

   _____

   _____

   _____

   _____

2. Point to words and phrases in the text that suggest the game in which Robert is a boar is dangerously close to out of control. What emotions do Robert and Ralph feel during the game?

   _____

   _____

   _____

   _____

3. How does the author use this passage to hint that the boys are reverting to a more primitive state of being? Cite specific textual evidence.

   _____

   _____

   _____

4. What inferences can you make about possible future events based on the actions and dialogue of the characters during this episode?

   _____

   _____

   _____

   _____

Name _____

Date _____

Making Connections– Organizing Causes and Effects

Directions: Working independently or with a partner, organize key events from chapters 6 and 7 into a cause-and-effect chart. The first causes and effects have been done for you. Complete at least five additional causes and effects on your chart.

Cause	Effect
A paratrooper is shot down during the war.	The dead paratrooper comes to rest on the island near the top of the mountain.
Samneric spot the dead paratrooper while tending the fire.	Samneric panic and run down to the camp.

Name _____

Date _____

Creating with the Story Elements

Directions: Thinking about the story elements of character, setting, and plot in a novel is very important to understanding what is happening and why. Complete **one** of the following activities based on what you've read so far. Be creative and have fun!

Characters

If you could send a care package to one of the novel's characters, what seven items would you include? Why? Create or draw a seven-item care package for your chosen character. Include an explanation of why you selected each of the items in the care package.

Setting

Imagine that you are standing in a specific location on the island. Where are you? What do you see, hear, smell, taste, and feel?

Plot

Create a soundtrack for chapters 6 and 7 of *Lord of the Flies*. Identify the various scenes in these chapters, and select a song that you think fits each scene. Then, write a brief explanation of why you made your selections.

Teacher Plans

Vocabulary Overview

Ten key words from this section are provided below with definitions and sentences about how the words are used in the book. Choose one of the vocabulary activity sheets (pages 45 or 46) for students to complete as they read this section. Monitor students as they work to ensure the definitions they have found are accurate and relate to the text. Finally, discuss these important vocabulary words with students. If you think these words or other words in the section warrant more time devoted to them, there are suggestions in the introduction for other vocabulary activities (page 5).

Word	Definition	Sentence about Text
prefect (ch. 8)	a senior student who is allowed to enforce discipline at a school	Jack claims Ralph has no right to give orders to the others because he is not a **prefect**.
derisive (ch. 8)	filled with contempt or ridicule	Piggy gives Simon a **derisive** look after Simon suggests climbing the mountain to learn about the beast.
cynicism (ch. 8)	skepticism; mistrust; a belief that people have selfish motivations	In Simon's imagination, the Lord of the Flies has a look of **cynicism** on its face.
taboo (ch. 8)	a practice, word, or topic of discussion that is forbidden	Ralph and Piggy stop mentioning Jack because his name has become almost **taboo**.
clamorously (ch. 9)	with noisy confusion	When Jack begins his beast-killing dance, the others join in **clamorously**.
superficial (ch. 9)	existing only on the surface, not underneath	At first, the dancing boys' excitement is only **superficial**.
phosphorescence (ch. 9)	a glowing light emitted without heat	In the darkness, the edge of the lagoon glows with **phosphorescence**.
interrogative (ch. 10)	questioning	A boy raises his finger in an **interrogative** way before asking a question about the Beast.
theological (ch. 10)	having to do with religion and beliefs about God	The boys have a **theological** discussion about how to appease the evil creature they have invented.
bowstave (ch. 10)	a trimmed rod of wood to be made into a shooting bow	The curved edge of the beach is described as having the appearance of a **bowstave**.

Name _____

Date _____

Understanding Vocabulary Words

Directions: The following words appear in this section of the book. Use context clues and reference materials to determine an accurate definition for each word.

Word	Definition
prefect (ch. 8)	
derisive (ch. 8)	
cynicism (ch. 8)	
taboo (ch. 8)	
clamorously (ch. 9)	
superficial (ch. 9)	
phosphorescence (ch. 9)	
interrogative (ch. 10)	
theological (ch. 10)	
bowstave (ch. 10)	

Name _____

Date _____

During-Reading Vocabulary Activity

Directions: As you read these chapters, record at least eight important words on the lines. Try to find interesting, difficult, intriguing, special, or funny words. Your words can be long or short. They can be hard or easy to spell. After each word, use context clues in the text and reference materials to define the word.

- _____
- _____
- _____
- _____
- _____
- _____
- _____
- _____
- _____

Directions: Respond to these questions about the words in this section.

1. Whose name has it become **taboo** for Ralph and Piggy to say? Why?

   _____
   _____
   _____
   _____

2. Why might an adult be more likely than a child to have **cynicism**?

   _____
   _____
   _____
   _____

Analyzing the Literature

Provided below are discussion questions you can use in small groups, with the whole class, or for written assignments. Each question is given at two levels so you can choose the right question for each group of students. Activity sheets with these questions are provided (pages 48–49) if you want students to write their responses. For each question, a few key discussion points are provided for your reference.

Story Element	■ Level 1	▲ Level 2	Key Discussion Points
Character	Contrast Jack's leadership style with Ralph's. How does Jack's "tribe" differ from the group led by Ralph?	Describe some ways in which the boys are regressing with Jack as their leader. How is the new "tribe" led by Jack more medieval or primitive?	Jack as "chief" is a dictator, whereas Ralph is more of a democratic leader. Jack orders the others to serve him and has boys beaten for no apparent reason. In chapter 9, he is sitting "painted and garlanded" above the others, looking "like an idol." He suggests primitive practices such as the leaving of the head as a sacrifice.
Plot	Why is Simon killed? Explain how weather, time of day, and location play roles in the death.	How do weather conditions and other factors of setting play a role in Simon's death? Could the death have been prevented?	The boys are already in a fearful and frenzied state when Simon crawls toward them. It is dark, and the weather is frightening. Simon's appearance has been altered by sweat, dirt, blood, and his seizure. Students may argue that a change in any of these factors could have affected the outcome.
Character	Which boys realize that Simon is the "Beast" they kill? Do some of the boys not know?	Does Jack believe in the "Beast"? Does he know that Simon is the killed "Beast"? What makes you think so?	Piggy and Ralph admit that they know the "Beast" is Simon. Arguably, Jack knows as well, since he is still suggesting strategies for appeasing the "Beast," even after it has ostensibly been killed. Students may argue that Jack is using the fear generated by the concept of a "Beast" to control the others.
Plot	Why do Jack and his followers raid the shelters in chapter 10?	What motives lie behind the nighttime raid on the shelters? Is it significant that the boys do not steal the conch?	The raid is an act of terrorism. It seems intended to demoralize and weaken those who Jack sees as his opposition. The failure to take the conch is significant in that it shows that Jack's group is not a democracy and places no value on this symbol of democracy.

Name _____

Date _____

Analyzing the Literature

Directions: Think about the section you just read. Read each question, and state your response with textual evidence.

1. Contrast Jack's leadership style with Ralph's. How does Jack's "tribe" differ from the group led by Ralph?

   _____

   _____

   _____

   _____

   _____

2. Why is Simon killed? Explain how weather, time of day, and location play roles in the death.

   _____

   _____

   _____

   _____

   _____

3. Which boys realize that Simon is the "Beast" they kill? Do some of the boys not know?

   _____

   _____

   _____

   _____

   _____

4. Why do Jack and his followers raid the shelters in chapter 10?

   _____

   _____

   _____

   _____

   _____

Name _____

Date _____

▲ Analyzing the Literature

Directions: Think about the section you just read. Read each question, and state your response with textual evidence.

1. Describe some ways in which the boys are regressing with Jack as their leader. How is the new "tribe" led by Jack more medieval or primitive?

_____
_____
_____
_____
_____
_____

2. How do weather conditions and other factors of setting play a role in Simon's death? Could the death have been prevented?

_____
_____
_____
_____

3. Does Jack believe in the "Beast"? Does he know that Simon is the killed "Beast"? What makes you think so?

_____
_____
_____
_____

4. What motives lie behind the nighttime raid on the shelters? Is it significant that the boys do not steal the conch?

_____
_____
_____
_____
_____
_____

Name _____

Date _____

Reader Response

Directions: Choose one of the following prompts about this section to answer. Be sure you include a topic sentence in your response, use textual evidence to support your opinion, and provide a strong conclusion that summarizes your opinion.

Writing Prompts

- **Argument Piece**—Why do most of the boys leave Ralph's camp and join Jack's? Describe at least three reasons this happens. Rank the reasons from most to least important and explain your rankings.
- **Narrative Piece**—Describe a time when you felt you had to choose between two or more different social groups. How were the groups different? What factors influenced your decision? Connect your decision-making process with that of the boys in *Lord of the Flies*.

_____

_____

_____

_____

_____

_____

_____

_____

_____

_____

_____

_____

_____

_____

_____

Close Reading the Literature

Directions: Closely reread the sections in which Simon sees and speaks to the "Lord of the Flies" in chapter 8. The first section begins, "Simon stayed where he was, a small brown image, concealed by the leaves." Continue until you read, "In Simon's right temple, a pulse began to beat on the brain." The second section begins, "You are a silly little boy." Continue until the end of the chapter. Read each question, and then revisit the text to find evidence that supports your answer.

1. What is the Lord of the Flies, and why is it there? Where in the text does Simon name or otherwise show awareness of what this object really is.

   _____

   _____

   _____

   _____

2. Based on the text, what factor(s) may be causing Simon to hallucinate?

   _____

   _____

3. What tone does the Lord of the Flies take when speaking to Simon? How would you characterize its personality? Use specific words and phrases to support your assertions.

   _____

   _____

   _____

4. What does the Lord of the Flies symbolize to Simon or in the larger context of the book? Explain how the text helps you draw this conclusion.

   _____

   _____

   _____

   _____

Name _____

Date _____

Making Connections–Text-to-Self, Text-to-Text, Text-to-World

Directions: Consider the events in chapters 8–10 of *Lord of the Flies*. Read the prompts. Select a prompt, and respond to it on the lines provided. Use examples from the text to support your answer.

Text-to-Self

Explain how something you've read about in chapters 8–10 of *Lord of the Flies* relates to your own life.

Text-to-Text

Describe a book or article you've read or a non-print text, such as a film or TV program, you've seen. Explain how this print or non-print text is related to chapters 8–10 of *Lord of the Flies*.

Text-to-World

Describe something that has recently happened or is happening in your community, country, or the world. Explain how this event is connected to what you've just read in chapters 8–10 of *Lord of the Flies*.

_____
_____
_____
_____
_____
_____
_____
_____
_____
_____
_____
_____

Name _____

Date _____

Creating with the Story Elements

Directions: Thinking about the story elements of character, setting, and plot in a novel is very important to understanding what is happening and why. Complete **one** of the following activities based on what you've read so far. Be creative and have fun!

Characters

Writing as Jack, create a numbered list of steps for overthrowing a democracy and becoming a dictator. Alternatively, writing as Piggy or Ralph, make a numbered list of steps for preventing dictatorial overthrow and preserving democracy.

Setting

Imagine that a hotel magically appears on the island and the boys can stay there the night of the storm. How might the plot of the novel change?

Plot

Dress up as a painted "savage" and take a photo. Then, photograph yourself in the most "civilized" clothing you can find. (Alternatively, you can use photo editing programs on existing photos to look more "savage" and more "civilized.") Mount your two photos together, and write about how you feel when looking at them.

Teacher Plans

Vocabulary Overview

Ten key words from this section are provided below with definitions and sentences about how the words are used in the book. Choose one of the vocabulary activity sheets (pages 55 or 56) for students to complete as they read this section. Monitor students as they work to ensure the definitions they have found are accurate and relate to the text. Finally, discuss these important vocabulary words with students. If you think these words or other words in the section warrant more time devoted to them, there are suggestions in the introduction for other vocabulary activities (page 5).

Word	Definition	Sentence about Text
myopia (ch. 11)	nearsightedness	Piggy's **myopia** makes it difficult for him to see without his glasses.
propitiatingly (ch. 11)	done in an effort to win favor or make someone less angry	When Ralph becomes defensive and loud, Piggy calms him by speaking **propitiatingly**.
ludicrous (ch. 11)	so out of place as to be laughable; ridiculous	Piggy dramatically clings to the rock in a way that appears **ludicrous** and laughable to the other boys.
truculently (ch. 11)	in an aggressive or defiant way; eager to fight	Jack and Ralph stare at each other **truculently** before coming to blows.
parried (ch. 11)	warded off a weapon or attack with a countermove	Ralph **parries** the blow Jack delivers with a spear.
talisman (ch. 11)	an object thought to have magic powers or bring luck	The conch shell has become a **talisman** to Piggy and Ralph.
inimical (ch. 12)	unfriendly; hostile	Ralph has to speak softly so that his presence won't be detected by the **inimical** savages nearby.
ululation (ch. 12)	a long, high-pitched tongue trill	When Eric beats on his open mouth, he is able to vocalize a faint **ululation**.
cordon (ch. 12)	a line of people enclosing an area	Ralph wonders if it would be wiser to climb a tree or charge through the **cordon**.
crepitation (ch. 12)	a crackling or rattling sound	Ralph can hear a **crepitation** as the fire begins to spread.

Name _____

Date _____

Understanding Vocabulary Words

Directions: The following words appear in this section of the book. Use context clues and reference materials to determine an accurate definition for each word.

Word	Definition
myopia (ch. 11)	
propitiatingly (ch. 11)	
ludicrous (ch. 11)	
truculently (ch. 11)	
parried (ch. 11)	
talisman (ch. 11)	
inimical (ch. 12)	
ululation (ch. 12)	
cordon (ch. 12)	
crepitation (ch. 12)	

Name _____

Date _____

During-Reading Vocabulary Activity

Directions: As you read these chapters, choose five important words from the story. Then, use those five words to complete this word flow chart. On each arrow, write a vocabulary word. In the boxes between the words, explain how the words connect. An example has been done for you using the words *ululations* and *cordon*.

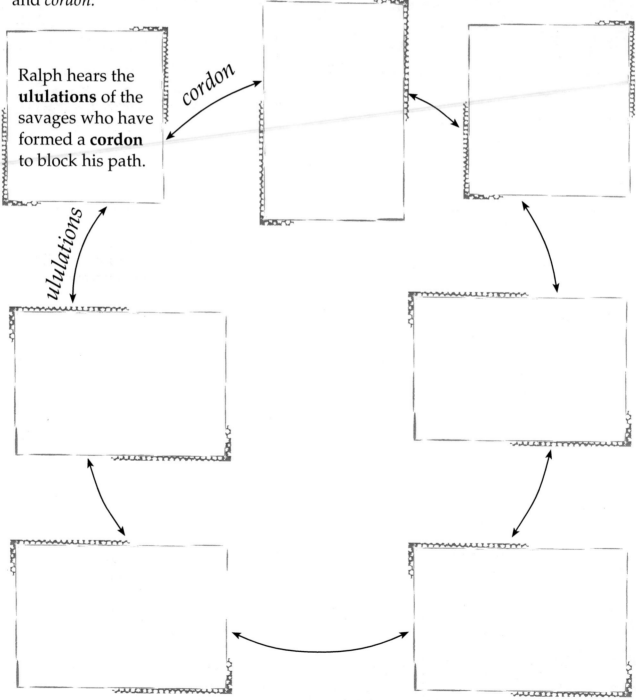

Analyzing the Literature

Provided below are discussion questions you can use in small groups, with the whole class, or for written assignments. Each question is given at two levels so you can choose the right question for each group of students. Activity sheets with these questions are provided (pages 58–59) if you want students to write their responses. For each question, a few key discussion points are provided for your reference.

Story Element	■ Level 1	▲ Level 2	Key Discussion Points
Setting	How has "Castle Rock" become like an actual medieval castle in chapter 11?	Discuss the role that "Castle Rock" plays in the chapter 11 action. How has its name become more significant?	"Castle Rock" has become like a medieval fortress. It has guards, a narrow passage leading to it, and defenses (the levered rock). It is high up and made of stone. The distance between Roger and the boys below depersonalizes them and makes it easier for Roger to release the killing boulder.
Character	How are Piggy and the conch connected? What happens to them in chapter 11, and why?	What does the destruction of the conch symbolize, and how and why is it linked to Piggy's murder?	Piggy has been the character who has most often mentioned and invoked the power of the conch. He is a human representative of reason, responsibility, and democratic governance, also represented by the conch. The other boys violently reject democracy and reason by destroying Piggy and the conch.
Plot	Do you think the hunt for Ralph could have ever happened if the pig hunting had not happened first? Why or why not?	How does hunting pigs create conditions that make the hunting of a human (Ralph) possible? Compare and contrast the pig hunt with the manhunt.	We see a gradual progression from hunting pigs to hunting Ralph. At first, even Jack cannot bring himself to kill a pig. Later, the boys slaughter pigs with relish, even a sow with piglets. The necessity of killing for food becomes the thrill of tormenting and killing another human to assert power.
Plot	How are the other boys harming themselves and the island as they work to harm Ralph? Why don't they stop?	In what ways does the manhunt destroy the island, and how is this destruction symbolic and important?	In their craze to kill Ralph, the boys set fire to the island, endangering themselves and destroying their sources of food and shelter. The destruction of the island paradise mirrors a fall from innocence into evil. Ironically, the boys who could not be bothered to tend to a signal fire, attract a ship with the smoke.

Name _____

Date _____

Analyzing the Literature

Directions: Think about the section you just read. Read each question, and state your response with textual evidence.

1. How has "Castle Rock" become like an actual medieval castle in chapter 11?

_____
_____
_____
_____

2. How are Piggy and the conch connected? What happens to them in chapter 11, and why?

_____
_____
_____
_____

3. Do you think the hunt for Ralph could have ever happened if the pig hunting had not happened first? Why or why not?

_____
_____
_____
_____

4. How are the other boys harming themselves and the island as they work to harm Ralph? Why don't they stop?

_____
_____
_____
_____

Name _____

Date _____

▲ Analyzing the Literature

Directions: Think about the section you just read. Read each question, and state your response with textual evidence.

1. Discuss the role that "Castle Rock" plays in the chapter 11 action. How has its name become more significant?

   _____

   _____

   _____

   _____

   _____

2. What does the destruction of the conch symbolize, and how and why is it linked to Piggy's murder?

   _____

   _____

   _____

   _____

   _____

3. How does hunting pigs create conditions that make the hunting of a human (Ralph) possible? Compare and contrast the pig hunt with the manhunt.

   _____

   _____

   _____

   _____

   _____

4. In what ways does the manhunt destroy the island, and how is this destruction symbolic and important?

   _____

   _____

   _____

   _____

   _____

Name _____

Date _____

Reader Response

Directions: Choose one of the following prompts about this section to answer. Be sure you include a topic sentence in your response, use textual evidence to support your opinion, and provide a strong conclusion that summarizes your opinion.

Writing Prompts

- **Argument Piece**—What view of human nature does this novel ultimately put forward? Do you agree with that view? Why or why not?
- **Informative/Explanatory Piece**—Discuss some of the ways that pigs and the word *pig* are significant in these chapters and throughout *Lord of the Flies*. Which characters are called pigs? Which characters are treated like pigs? What do pigs symbolize?

_____

_____

_____

_____

_____

_____

_____

_____

_____

_____

_____

_____

_____

_____

_____

_____

_____

_____

_____

Name _____

Date _____

Close Reading the Literature

Directions: Closely reread the final pages of the novel, beginning with the sentence, "The cries, suddenly nearer, jerked him up." Read each question, and then revisit the text to find evidence that supports your answer.

1. What is significant about the stick held by the savage who finds Ralph? How is it described? What inference does the author want you to make about Ralph's potential fate based on the appearance of the stick?

   _____
   _____
   _____
   _____

2. How has Ralph become like a pig? Point to specific words and phrases that suggest Ralph's similarity to a hunted pig.

   _____
   _____
   _____
   _____

3. Contrast the way Ralph views the other boys while he is being hunted with the way the officer views the boys on the final pages of the book. Include specific details from the text that support your assertions.

   _____
   _____
   _____
   _____

4. How are the boys changed by the entrance onto the scene of an adult authority figure? Cite textual evidence in your answer.

   _____
   _____
   _____
   _____

Name _____

Date _____

Making Connections–*Lord of the Flies* as a World War II Novel

Author William Golding was deeply affected by the experience of living through—and fighting in—World War II. Some critics have seen a parallel between Jack's rise to power in *Lord of the Flies* and Hitler's rise to power in Germany.

Directions: Read the statements about Hitler and Nazi Germany. Then, connect each event with an event or series of events from *Lord of the Flies*.

1. Hitler gave brilliant speeches that inspired people.

   _____

   _____

   _____

2. Germany was in a depression. Hitler promised to give people things they needed.

   _____

   _____

   _____

3. Hitler murdered and persecuted Jewish people, Gypsies, and others perceived as "different" or "outsiders."

   _____

   _____

   _____

4. On a night called *Kristallnacht*, Jewish neighborhoods were raided and terrorized, people were killed, and buildings were destroyed.

   _____

   _____

   _____

5. People were afraid to stand up and speak out against Hitler because he persecuted and killed those who opposed him.

   _____

   _____

   _____

Creating with the Story Elements

Directions: Thinking about the story elements of character, setting, and plot in a novel is very important to understanding what is happening and why. Complete **one** of the following activities based on what you've read so far. Be creative and have fun!

Characters

Write an obituary for Piggy or Simon. Include a list of best qualities and lifetime accomplishments.

Setting

Create a collage or abstract painting that includes images of the natural objects and/or forces that play important roles in the last two chapters of *Lord of the Flies*.

Plot

Pretend to be a news reporter and report "live" from one of the scenes in chapters 11 and 12 of *Lord of the Flies*. Record your report, and share it with your friends or with your class.

Name _____

Date _____

Post-Reading Theme Thoughts

Directions: Read each of the statements in the first column. Choose a main character from *Lord of the Flies*. Think about that character's point of view. From that character's perspective, decide if the character would agree or disagree with the statements. Record the character's opinion by marking an X in Agree or Disagree for each statement. Explain your choices in the fourth column using textual evidence.

Character I Chose: _____

Statement	Agree	Disagree	Explain Your Answer
Those perceived as different are more likely to be picked on and become scapegoats.			
Children by nature are not moral. They need adults to teach and reinforce moral behavior.			
In the absence of laws and social structures, human beings will slip into a state of cruel savagery.			
Honesty is the best policy.			

Name _____

Date _____

Culminating Activity:
Write a *Lord of the Flies* Reunion Story

Directions: Imagine two or more of the characters from *Lord of the Flies* meeting again as teens or adults. How might they meet? What might the characters be like? What would they say to one another? How would they feel about their shared past on the island? Write a story in which two or more surviving characters are somehow reunited.

_____

_____

_____

_____

_____

_____

_____

_____

_____

_____

_____

_____

_____

_____

_____

_____

_____

_____

_____

_____

_____

Name _____

Date _____

Culminating Activity:
Create a *Lord of the Flies* Movie Poster or Trailer

Directions: Imagien you are a director making a movie of *Lord of the Flies*. How would you promote it? Create either a movie poster or a movie trailer to promote your film of *Lord of the Flies*.

Movie Poster

Decide who you would cast for the major roles, and include information about the actors on the poster.

Include a paragraph of text that introduces the concept of the movie and builds interest without giving away too much about what happens at the climax of the movie.

Include one or more quotations from reviewers. (You can make these up.)

Make your poster visually intriguing so that it will inspire viewers to want to see the movie.

Movie Trailer

Keep your movie trailer under two and a half minutes in length.

Movie trailers typically include a number of different scenes or shots taken from the upcoming movie. Include at least three different scenes or shots in your trailer.

Include a voice-over that gives some information about the movie and creates suspense and/or builds interest. The voice-over might also include information about actors playing various roles.

Do not give away too much about what happens at the climax and ending of the movie. In other words, no spoilers.

Name _____

Date _____

Comprehension Assessment

Directions: Circle the letter for the best response to each question.

1. In *Lord of the Flies*, which of the following symbolic objects is most closely associated with a democratic system of government?

    A. the pig's head

    B. Jack's choir cap

    C. Piggy's glasses

    D. the conch shell

2. What event is foreshadowed when Jack, Ralph, and Simon push down a huge boulder in chapter 1 of *Lord of the Flies*?

    A. the naval officer's arrival

    B. the death of Piggy

    C. the construction of shelters

    D. the burning of the island

3. What does Piggy view as the group's most important activity?

    A. hunting for meat

    B. building a raft

    C. exploring the island

    D. maintaining a fire

4. Which of the following statements summarizes a major theme of *Lord of the Flies*?

    A. The innocence of children is a beautiful thing.

    B. A civilization that wastes too many resources caring for the weak cannot survive.

    C. Human beings are capable of great evil.

    D. Camping adventures build character in young people.

Comprehension Assessment (cont.)

5. Which of the following quotations from the novel provides support to your answer from question 4?

    E. "You'll get back to where you came from."

    F. "Maybe there is a Beast....What I mean is...maybe it's only us."

    G. "While we're waiting we can have a good time on this island."

    H. "All day I've been working with Simon. No one else. They're off bathing, or eating, or playing."

6. Which major character is being described in the following passage from *Lord of the Flies*?

    "[He] was sitting there, naked to the waist, his face blocked out in white and red. The tribe lay in a semicircle before him. The newly beaten and untied Wilfred was sniffing noisily in the background."

    A. Jack

    B. Ralph

    C. Simon

    D. the Lord of the Flies

7. Explain why the character description in question 6 is significant in terms of the major themes of the novel.

    _____

    _____

    _____

    _____

    _____

    _____

8. Which of the following statements about the Lord of the Flies is true?

    A. The Lord of the Flies is a name the other boys give to Jack.

    B. The Lord of the Flies is a pig's head on a stake.

    C. Piggy dreams that the Lord of the Flies is speaking to him.

    D. Ralph and Piggy carry the Lord of the Flies to Castle Rock.

Name _____

Date _____

Response to Literature:
The Universe in *Lord of the Flies*

Directions: In his 1962 introduction to *Lord of the Flies*, novelist E. M. Forster praised the novel by saying that in it, author William Golding "presents the universe, under the guise of a school adventure story on a coral island." Explain what you think Forster meant by this. Then, explain whether you agree or disagree with Forster.

_____

_____

_____

_____

_____

_____

_____

_____

_____

_____

_____

_____

_____

_____

_____

_____

_____

_____

_____

_____

_____

_____

Name _____

Date _____

Response to Literature Rubric

Directions: Use this rubric to evaluate student responses.

	Exceptional Writing	Quality Writing	Developing Writing
Focus and Organization	☐ States a clear opinion and elaborates well. Engages the reader from the opening hook through the middle to the conclusion. Demonstrates clear understanding of the intended audience and purpose of the piece.	☐ Provides a clear and consistent opinion. Maintains a clear perspective and supports it through elaborating details. Makes the opinion clear in the opening hook and summarizes well in the conclusion.	☐ Provides an inconsistent point of view. Does not support the topic adequately or misses pertinent information. Provides lack of clarity in the beginning, middle, and conclusion.
Text Evidence	☐ Provides comprehensive and accurate support. Includes relevant and worthwhile text references.	☐ Provides limited support. Provides few supporting text references.	☐ Provides very limited support for the text. Provides no supporting text references.
Written Expression	☐ Uses descriptive and precise language with clarity and intention. Maintains a consistent voice and uses an appropriate tone that supports meaning. Uses multiple sentence types and transitions well between ideas.	☐ Uses a broad vocabulary. Maintains a consistent voice and supports a tone and feelings through language. Varies sentence length and word choices.	☐ Uses a limited and unvaried vocabulary. Provides an inconsistent or weak voice and tone. Provides little to no variation in sentence type and length.
Language Conventions	☐ Capitalizes, punctuates, and spells accurately. Demonstrates complete thoughts within sentences, with accurate subject-verb agreement. Uses paragraphs appropriately and with clear purpose.	☐ Capitalizes, punctuates, and spells accurately. Demonstrates complete thoughts within sentences and appropriate grammar. Paragraphs are properly divided and supported.	☐ Incorrectly capitalizes, punctuates, and spells. Uses fragmented or run-on sentences. Utilizes poor grammar overall. Paragraphs are poorly divided and developed.

The responses provided here are just examples of what students may answer. Many accurate responses are possible for the questions throughout this unit.

During-Reading Vocabulary Activity—Section 1:
Chapters 1–2 (page 16)

1. The word **scar** is used to describe the rip in the forest caused by the crash landing of the boys' plane.

2. The word **decorous** is used to describe Piggy, who behaves in a polite, restrained way.

Close Reading the Literature—Section 1:
Chapters 1–2 (page 21)

1. Possible sentences include: "When his party was about ten yards from the platform he shouted an order and they halted…." Jack has authority over the choir boys, who may not necessarily like him but obey him.

2. "Inside the floating cloak he was tall, thin, and bony; and his hair was red beneath the black cap. His face was crumpled and freckled, and ugly without silliness. Out of this face stared two light blue eyes, frustrated now, and turning, or ready to turn, to anger." Jack does not sound attractive or pleasant in this description, which highlights his tendency to frustration and anger.

3. Piggy is "intimidated by this uniformed superiority and the offhand authority" of Jack, so he doesn't ask anyone for his name. Piggy "shrank to the other side of Ralph and busied himself with his glasses."

4. Piggy and Jack seem unlikely to become friends, since Jack is almost immediately abusive to Piggy, calling him "Fatty" and telling him to "Shut up." Jack and Ralph also perhaps seem unlikely to become friends, since Ralph is voted chief and Jack believes he should be in charge.

Making Connections—Section 1:
Chapters 1–2 (page 22)

1. The boys push the rock down just for the fun of watching it crash.

2. Students may predict that a falling boulder may eventually injure or kill one of the boys.

3. Students may predict that the boys will eventually kill and eat a pig.

4. The boys use the glasses to start a fire.

5. Students may predict the boys will need to continue to use the glasses for fire making.

6. Students may predict that the glasses will eventually be broken or lost.

7. They light a fire in order to attract a ship for rescue, but the fire gets out of control.

8. Students may predict that the boys will cause another wildfire later in the novel.

During-Reading Vocabulary Activity—Section 2:
Chapters 3–5 (page 26)

1. Jack and Simon are both described as **furtive** while in the jungle. Jack is attempting to track a pig, and Simon is going behind a "mat" of creepers to be alone.

2. Ralph is annoyed by Piggy's **footling** comments.

Close Reading the Literature—Section 2:
Chapters 3–5 (page 31)

1. "In his other life [he] had received chastisement for filling a younger eye with sand." Maurice has been conditioned to obey rules and feels "uneasy" disobeying, even with no adults present.

2. Roger sounds like a frightening and unpleasant character. He is described as having a "shock of black hair," a "gloomy face," and "an unsociable remoteness" that is almost "forbidding."

3. Roger is harassing, rather than hurting, Henry. He feels the "taboo" against harming those who would have been protected in his "old life" by "parents and school and policemen and the law."

4. Students may predict that in the extended absence of adults, the "taboo" against hurting other children will weaken, and the boys' treatment of one another will worsen.

Close Reading the Literature—Section 3:
Chapters 6–7 (page 41)

1. Ralph seems excited about wounding a boar. He feels the excitement of hunting for the first time. The text says that he "sunned himself in their new respect and felt that hunting was good after all."

2. Robert squeals first in "mock terror," then in "real pain." He clearly feels fear as he screams and struggles. Ralph finds himself wanting to "squeeze and hurt" Robert along with the others.

3. Maurice suggests turning the "game" with its killing chant into a sort of ceremony. He says it could be done more "properly" if the boys used a drum and had a fire. Jack suggests to "get someone to dress up as a pig." After Robert suggests using a real pig "because you've got to kill him," Jack replies to "use a littlun."

4. Students may predict that a child may later be seriously harmed or killed in a similar way.

During-Reading Vocabulary Activity—Section 4:
Chapters 8–10 (page 46)

1. Jack's name has become **taboo**. They are trying to avoid an unpleasant subject. Also, they may feel that discussing Jack, in some way, gives him more power.

2. An adult is more likely than a child to have **cynicism** because he or she may have seen examples of other people acting out of selfish motivations.

Close Reading the Literature—Section 4:
Chapters 8–10 (page 51)

1. The Lord of the Flies is literally a "pig's head on a stick," as Simon says. Jack and his followers have left it behind as a sort of primitive sacrifice meant to appease the "Beast."

2. Simon has some type of physical disorder, perhaps epilepsy, which gives him spells. In this section, he is dehydrated ("licking his dry lips") and having "a little headache." He then feels "a pulse" beating in his head and knows that "one of his times [is] coming on."

3. The Lord of the Flies speaks "in the voice of a schoolmaster." He is like an unkind adult in that he orders Simon around and laughs at him, calling him a "silly little boy."

4. The Lord of the Flies, whose eyes are "dim with the infinite cynicism of adult life," represents the opposite of innocence, the evil in humans, or even the devil. Simon seems to fall into a hellmouth at the chapter's end, and students can be introduced to hellmouth images from art history.

Close Reading the Literature—Section 5:
Chapters 11–12 (page 61)

1. The stick is "sharpened at both ends." This seems to imply that Ralph's head is going to end up on a stake, much like the pig's.

2. Ralph is worried that, like a pig, he will end up killed and with his head on a stake. He is hiding from hunters in the brush, like a pig. While he is hiding, "a herd of pigs [comes] squealing out of the greenery."

3. Ralph sees himself as hunted by a cunning and deadly "savage." Conversely, the officer sees a "semicircle of little boys, their bodies streaked with colored clay."

4. When Ralph claims to be "boss," Jack considers contradicting, but, in the officer's presence, does not. The boys seem to become children again. Though they previously seemed to be unfeeling and perhaps even excited about the manhunt, they now "shake and sob."

Making Connections—Section 5:
Chapters 11–12 (page 62)

1. Ralph loses his ability to inspire the others with speeches, while Jack dramatically makes promises that bring boys over to his "tribe."

2. Jack promises the hungry boys meat and fun times if they join him.

3. Piggy and Simon, two characters seen as different from the others, are targeted and killed in *Lord of the Flies*.

4. The terrorizing raid on the shelters at night may be seen as a sort of parallel to Kristallnacht.

5. Even Samneric end up betraying Ralph and participating in the manhunt because they are physically threatened and harmed, and they fear becoming similar targets themselves.

Comprehension Assessment
(pages 67–68)

1. D. the conch shell

2. B. the death of Piggy

3. D. maintaining a fire

4. C. Human beings are capable of great evil.

5. F. "Maybe there is a Beast….What I mean is…maybe it's only us."

6. A. Jack

7. The original democratic social order is gone, and Jack has become a dictator who uses fear and pain to enforce his will. The children are regressing into a more primitive state.

8. B. The Lord of the Flies is a pig's head on a stake.